MAKE AND COLOUR

Christmas DECORATIONS

Clare Beaton

b small publishing

How to use this book

Pull out the centre black and white pages of the book. These are ready-drawn decorations and cards for you to colour. **Cut along the solid lines and fold along the dotted lines.**

For colouring in, you can use coloured pencils, crayons, felt-tip pens or paints. Start colouring the centre of the decoration first. Leave edges until last so you don't smudge them.

Use fairly thick paint and wash your brush between colours. Leave the decorations flat to dry before folding along any dotted lines.

Keep the rest of the book. It has lots of other ideas on how to make your own decorations too.

On the inside back cover flap there are some festive stencil shapes. You will need these for some of the decorations in the book and you can also have fun making up your own.

Some things you will need:
★ plain and coloured paper and card
★ tissue paper and giftwrap
★ sequins and glitter
★ pencil and ruler
★ scissors and craft knife
★ glue
★ sticky tape
★ sticky shapes
★ crayons, paints and felt-tip pens
★ thread, wool and string

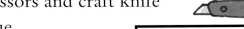

> **Be careful when using a craft knife.**

Templates

If you need to trace from either the dove template (on the inside front cover) or the templates on pages 6 and 7, here is how to do it very simply and successfully.

What you will need:
★ tracing paper
★ soft pencil
★ sticky tape
★ paper or card

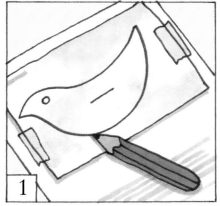
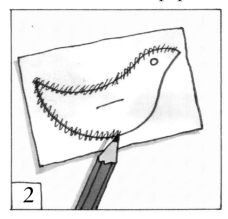

Trace the template shape with the pencil. Tape down the tracing paper to keep it still.

Turn over again and tape on to the card or paper. Retrace firmly over the lines. Remove the tracing paper.

Stencils

Cut along the perforated line and remove the sheet of stencils from the back cover of the book. Use them to make all kinds of different decorations. (See pages 6, 7, and 8 for ideas.

What you will need:
★ coloured paper or card, or Christmas giftwrap
★ pencil and scissors

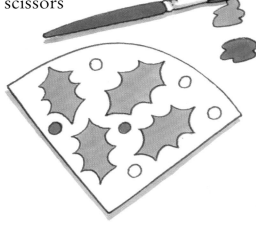

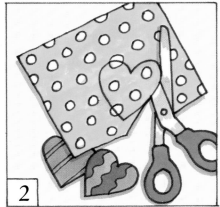

Place the stencil shape on the card or paper. Draw inside the shape with a pencil.

Cut out a few and use for decorations.

Or draw stencil on to a cut-out template shape like the cone on page 6 and colour it in.

Nativity scene

Make this simple background to stand behind your Nativity figures from the centre pull-out pages of the book.

Cut a strip of card about 40 cm x 21 cm. Draw the background picture of the stable and hills. Cut out the shapes along the top.

Be careful with a craft knife.

Paint and leave to dry.

← Score and fold.

Score with a craft knife on each side of the stable.

Score and fold. →

Use the stencil to make a star from paper. Dab with glue and then add glitter. Stick on the top of the stable.

Stick smaller sticky stars on the sky. Or use the stencil to draw and paint them.

Bend gently so the background will stand up.

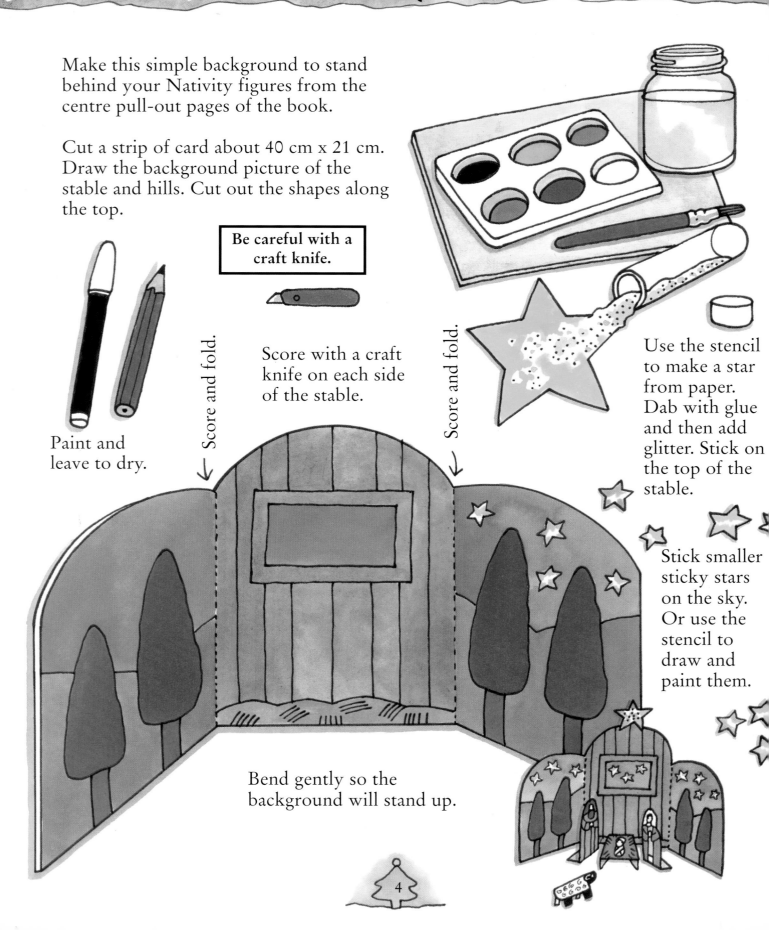

Nativity figures

Colour in the figures. Cut out and then fold along the dotted lines. Stand up in front of the Nativity background (see page 4).

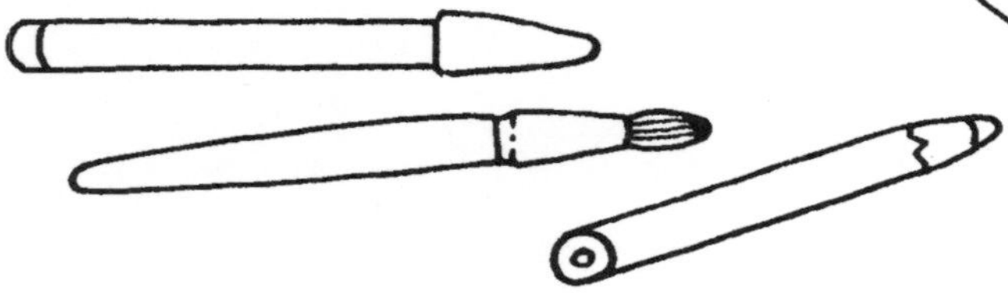

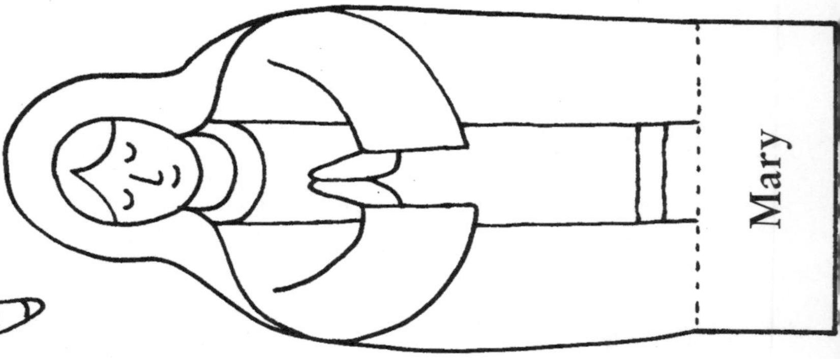

Mary

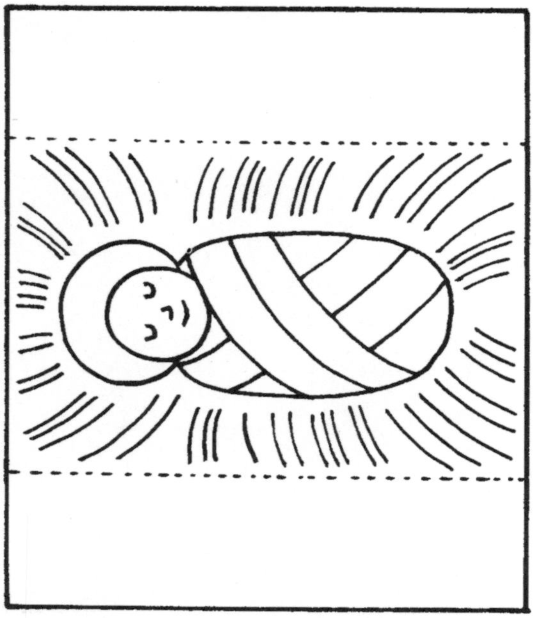

Joseph

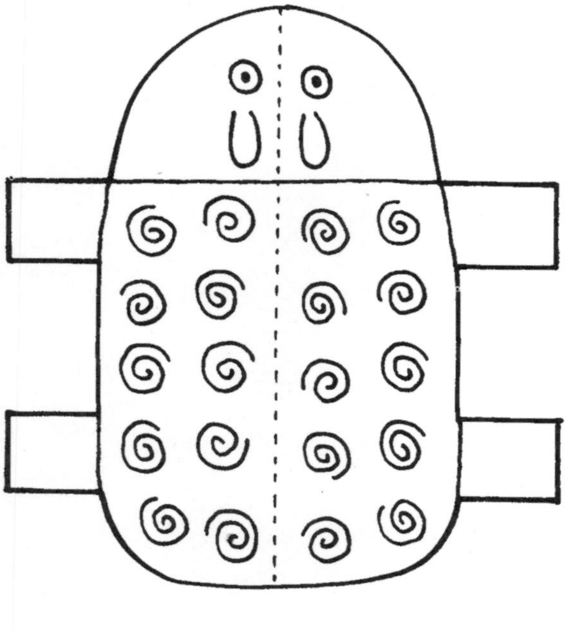

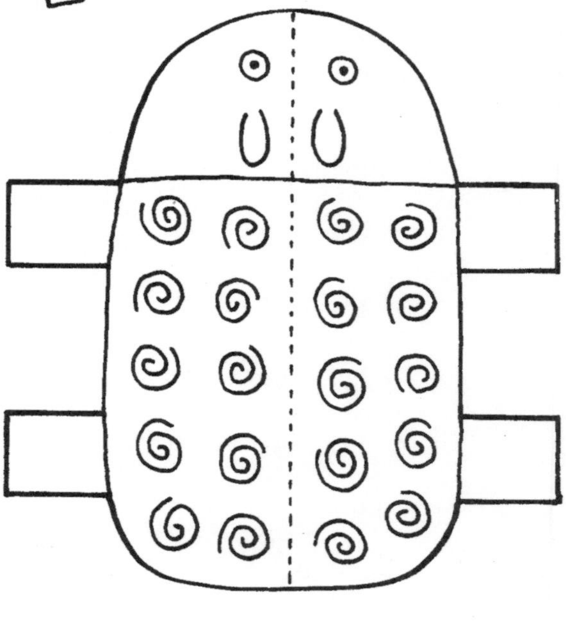

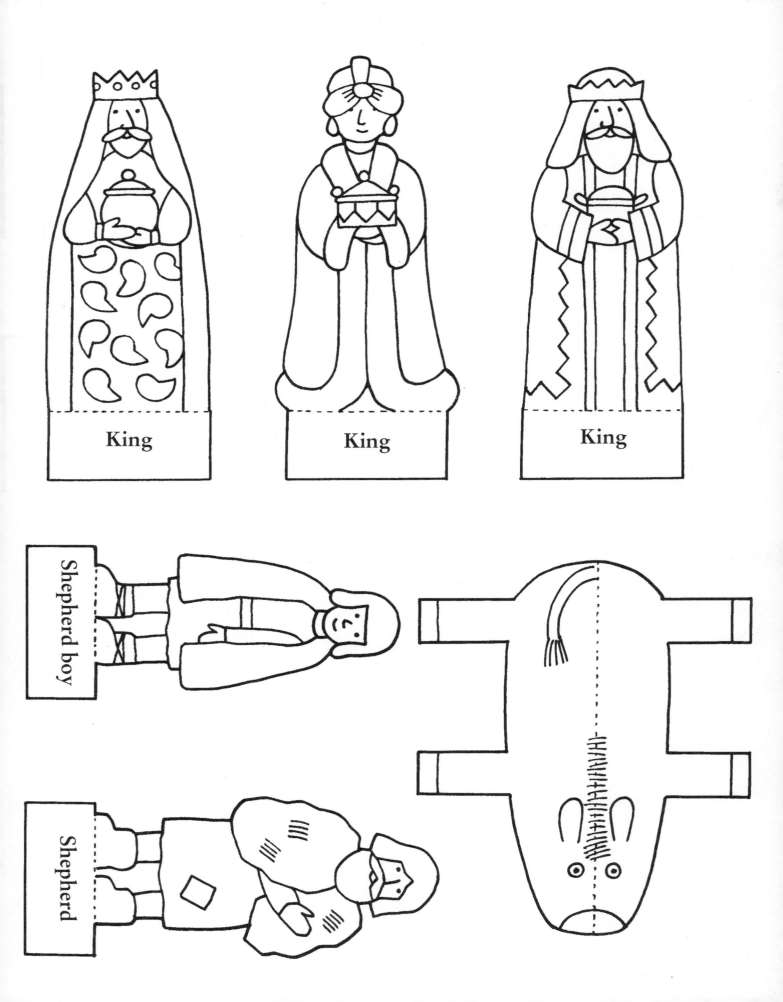

King

King

King

Shepherd boy

Shepherd

Christmas boxes
Colour the box. Cut out and fold it carefully along the dotted lines. Glue where marked and make into a box. Press glued edges together well.

Glue

Glue   Glue   Glue

Glue

Tape the ends of some wool inside the box to hang.

Glue   Glue   Glue

Glue

Put a tiny surprise inside the box – but it must be very light. Hang on the tree.

Standing cards
Colour in and decorate both sides of the cards. Cut out. Cut along the line down the centre of the cards. Slot together.

Snowflakes

Dab glue on to the snowflakes and sprinkle glitter on both sides. Cut out and cut down one line to the centre of each snowflake. Slot together.

Glue the end of wool or string to the top of the snowflake and hang up.

Christmas angel and fairy
Colour the figures or decorate them
with glue and glitter.

   Cut them out including the arms.
Curl the arms forward by pulling
carefully along closed scissors.

   Pull the skirt around to form cone
and secure with sticky tape on the
inside.

Christmas lanterns

Colour them and cut them out.
Fold in two lengthways. Cut along
the lines with scissors.

Pull together and tape the top and
bottom. Tape handle inside the top
and hang up.

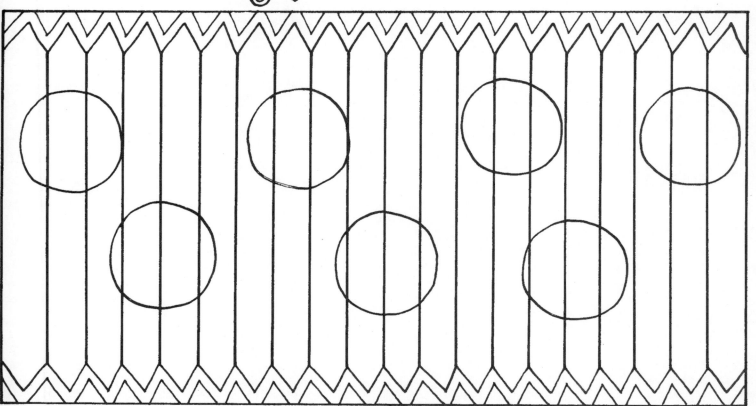

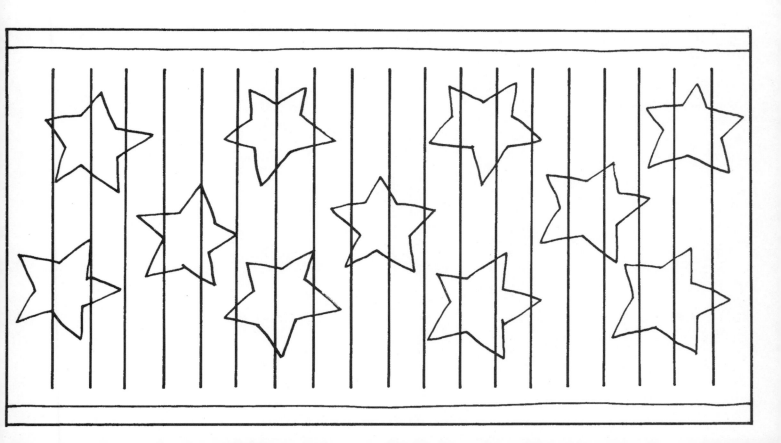

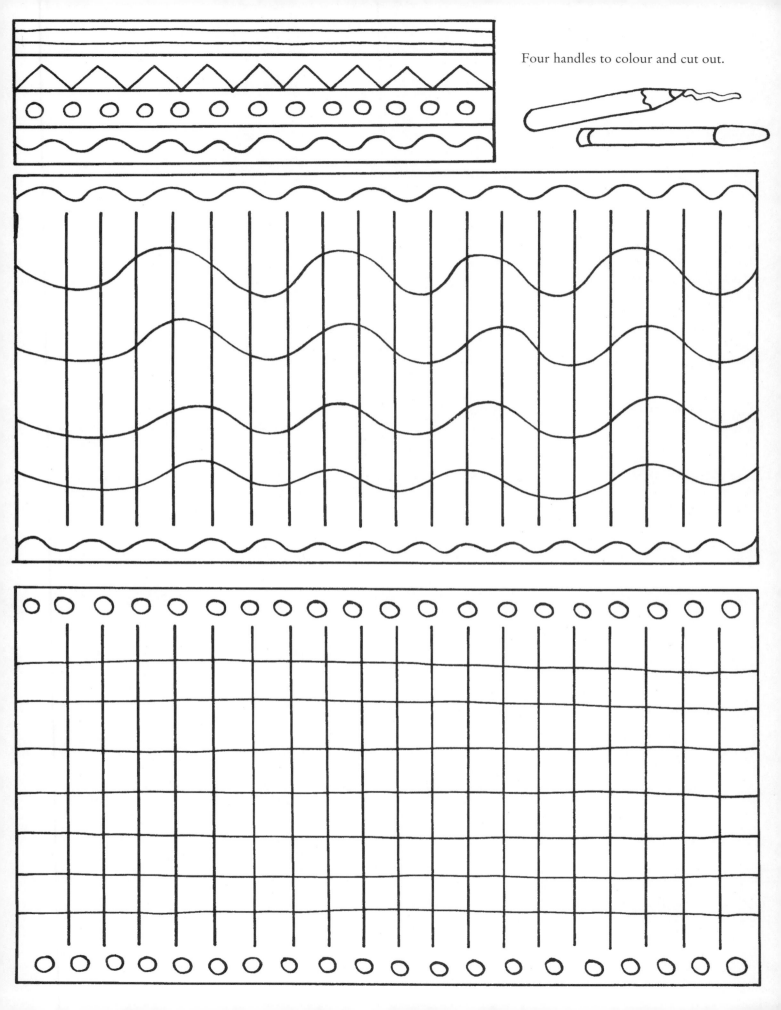

Four handles to colour and cut out.

Flying dove

Use the dove shape on the inside of the front cover. Follow the template instructions on page 3 to make this Christmas dove.

Make the dove from stiff white paper. Cut a slit in the centre.

Fold tissue paper into a concertina. Push it into the slit.

Dab glue on the body and sprinkle with glitter.

Cut a length of thread. Glue the top of the wings together with the end of the thread inside.

Hang up.

Christmas cone

These look very pretty hanging on the Christmas tree.

Use the template instructions on page 3 and trace the cone and handle outlines below on to coloured paper.
  Use the stencil at the back of the book to decorate with shapes. Or you can use sticky shapes, glue on sequins or draw on patterns with felt-tip pens.

Roll the paper into a cone. Secure with sticky tape. Glue the handle inside at the top.

Put sweets inside.

Cut the curved edge of the cone into different shapes.

scallops

zigzag

fringe

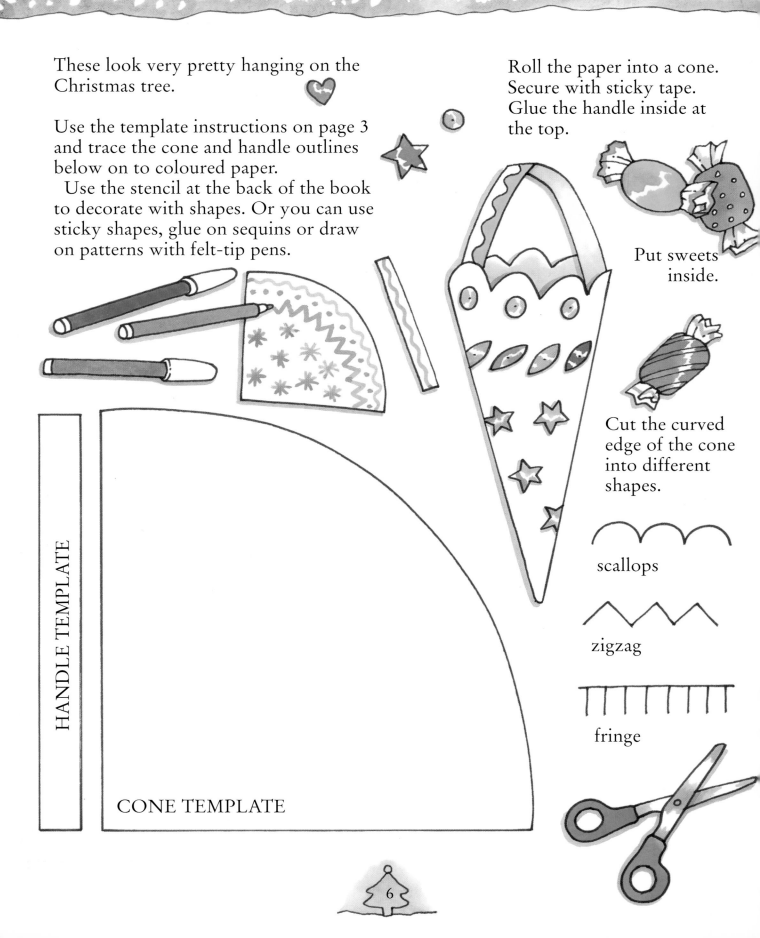

HANDLE TEMPLATE

CONE TEMPLATE

6

Napkin rings

Make a set of these Christmas napkin rings for parties or special holiday meals. If you use stiff paper, they can be used several times.

Use the template instructions on page 3 to draw this napkin ring shape on to stiff red or white paper. Cut it out.

Following the instructions on page 3, use the small holly leaf stencil to decorate the wreath. Then when it is dry, slot the two ends together to form the ring.

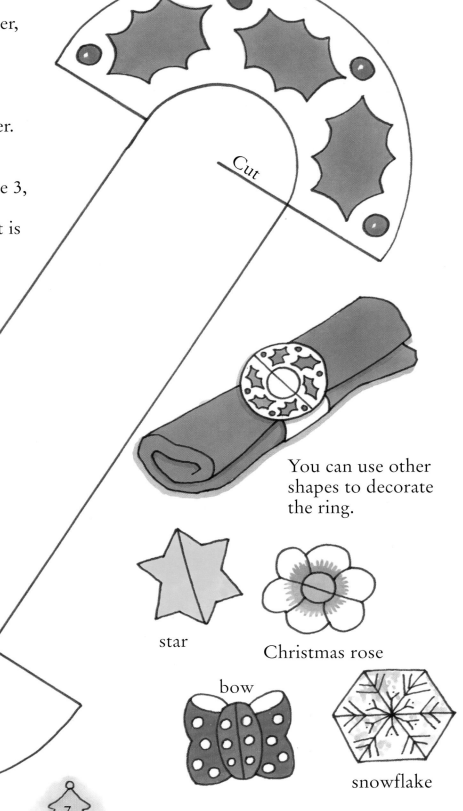

Cut

Cut

You can use other shapes to decorate the ring.

star

Christmas rose

bow

snowflake

Christmas streamers

Use the stencil shapes to make these pretty hanging garlands.

Follow the instructions on page 3 and draw inside the stencil shapes on to Christmas wrapping paper. You can use recycled giftwrap.

Glue half the shapes on the unpatterned side. Then put them in a row and lay a length of wool or thin string along the middle. Cover them with the other cut-out and glued shapes.

Paper chains

Using Christmas wrapping paper cut out strips measuring 20 cm x 3 cm.

Hang from a window or around a light shade.

Dab glue on one end of strips and link together to make chains.